Flue Covers

COLLECTOR'S VALUE GUIDE

Jim Meckley II

COLLECTOR BOOKS
A Division of Schroeder Publishing Co., Inc.

The current values in this book should be used only as a guide. They are not intended to set prices, which vary from one section of the country to another. Auction prices as well as dealer prices vary greatly and are affected by condition as well as demand. Neither the Author nor the Publisher assumes responsibility for any losses that might be incurred as a result of consulting this guide.

Searching For A Publisher?

We are always looking for knowledgeable people considered to be experts within their fields. If you feel that there is a real need for a book on your collectible subject and have a large comprehensive collection, contact Collector Books.

On The cover: A Pretty Bouquet, 9½", $85.00 – 95.00. Elizabeth, 9½", $85.00 – 95.00. A Fall Delight, 10", $65.00 – 75.00. Czarina, 9½", $90.00 – 100.00.

Cover design: Beth Summers
Book design: Joyce Cherry

Additional copies of this book may be ordered from:

COLLECTOR BOOKS
P.O. Box 3009
Paducah, Kentucky 42002-3009

@$12.95. Add $2.00 for postage and handling.

Contents

Dedication

This book is dedicated
to
my understanding and patient wife

Lillian

Acknowledgments

To Don and Cass Everhart for the use of their fine collection and their technical input.

To Barbara Sheffer, Bernard Figlock, and Chris Stetzer for use of part of their collections.

To Dana Shirey for her assistance and encouragement with the photography.

To Jim Meckley III for word processing and proofreading.

Introduction

In the past, when the heating season was finished for the warmer months of the year, a general house cleaning was undertaken. Along with this house cleaning came the removal of the stove pipes. What remained was a hole in the wall that the stovepipes had occupied. The device known as a flue cover was developed to cover this unsightly hole and was designed to dress up the area.

The covers were usually an attractive lithographed picture with various subjects, sandwiched between a piece of glass and a piece of cardboard. The entire picture and its covers were surrounded and held together by a metal rim.

Several types of rims were used. The most common was made of a narrow, soft piece of tin which was soldered at the joint. A similar, heavier style was made of the same material but was crimped like a pie curst, making it somewhat stronger.

Another style, more scarce than the others, was stamped from a flat sheet of brass, and then formed with a decorative pattern around the perimeter making it much stronger.

Most flue covers were round, ranging from 4¼" to 15¾" in diameter. Oval and diamond shapes can also be found.

Since the hook to retain the flue cover to the wall had to be above the flue hole, a chain fastened to the rim was added to facilitate hanging.

Some covers have been found stamped on the reverse side with Germany, Belgium, and Austria. However, no evidence has been uncovered indicating a manufacturer in the United States.

Flue covers were sometimes hung in groups of two or three to make a more attractive display. This is where the smaller flue covers of 4½" to 6" were used.

Flue covers were used in the 1890s through the 1930s and sold in five & dime stores such as W.T. Grant and McCrory's.

Very attractive reproductions are being produced today but are easily identified by the experienced collector.

Another style called a flue cap or stop had a broad metal rim, a picture in the center, and a spring arrangement on the back which expanded against the flue itself. These are listed in an 1897 Sears & Roebuck catalog, selling for four cents each. They may still be purchased today in some hardware stores. Examples of these may be found on page 6.

These can be found in several sizes and with a variety of scenes.

This three-dimensional figure of a cat is very unusual and uses the same type of installation.

Suggested Pricing

Prices shown are for flue covers in excellent condition. Missing or replaced chain, rim damage, water marks, and broken or missing glass will reduce values.

The subject of the picture can also affect pricing. Subjects that are cross collectible, such as black art, Santa Claus, or nursery rhymes, can be higher in value. Prices will vary considerably from area to area.

Kittens Caddy, 7¼" x 9", $70.00 – 80.00.

The Old Gray Mare, 7¾", $70.00 – 80.00.

Bear Facts, 8½",
$150.00 – 175.00.

Lassie, 9½",
$75.00 – 85.00.

Three Little Kittens, 9½",
$90.00 – 100.00.

A Game of Croquet,
9½", $100.00 – 110.00.

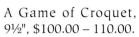

Sir Winston, 9½",
$70.00 – 80.00.

Kitten's Prey, 9½",
$90.00 – 100.00.

The Hunt, 9½",
$80.00 – 90.00.

Feeding King, 9½",
$75.00 – 85.00.

Feline Love, 7¾",
$90.00 – 100.00.

Resting with Storm,
9¼", $65.00 – 75.00.

Dark Town Strutters Ball, 9½",
$175.00 – 200.00.

Buddies,   9½",
$250.00 – 300.00.

The Fortune Teller, 9½",
$150.00 – 175.00.

Cherubs

Cherub and Stars, 8",
$55.00 – 60.00.

In the Garden, 14", $90.00 – 100.00.

The Cherub, 7½", has also been found 8" round and 7" x 8½" oval, $55.00 – 65.00.

Whispering Cherubs, 9¼",
$60.00 – 70.00.

Children

Linda's Fruit, 9½",
$75.00 – 85.00.

The Turban, 7¾",
$60.00 – 70.00.

The Pink Chapeau, 7¾",
$65.00 – 75.00.

Brother and Sister, 5¾",
$50.00 – 60.00.

The Blueboy, 8½",
$50.00 – 60.00.

Cutie, 8½",
$50.00 – 60.00.

Maria with Roses, 8½",
$85.00 – 95.00.

Just One Nanny?, 9¾" x
9¾", $75.00 – 85.00.

Daddy's Girls, 9½",
$60.00 – 70.00.

Blowing Bubbles, 7¾",
$50.00 – 60.00.

Peck's Bad Boy, 9¾",
$75.00 – 85.00.

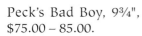

Rebecca in Red, 9½",
$90.00 – 100.00.

Adam's Fruit, 9½", also
found in 5" diameter,
$85.00 – 95.00.

Peri and Pixy, 9½", $80.00 – 90.00.

Branch of Cherries, 7" x 8½", $75.00 – 85.00.

Sabrina's Poppies, 8",
$75.00 – 85.00.

Alice Blue, 7¾",
$75.00 – 85.00.

The Ruffled Bonnet, 7¾",
$50.00 – 60.00.

Daisy, 7³/₄",
$50.00 – 60.00.

Green Biretta, 4¾",
$55.00 – 65.00.

Wintertime, 5¾",
$55.00 – 65.00.

Wig Children, 11¾",
$65.00 – 75.00.

The Blue Bonnet, 7¾",
$50.00 – 60.00.

A Blue Bouquet, 7¾",
$50.00 – 60.00.

The Young Master, 7¾",
$50.00 – 60.00.

Dressed for Sunday, 7¾",
$50.00 – 60.00.

Young Julianna, 7¾",
$50.00 – 60.00.

Garden Tease, 7½",
$75.00 – 85.00.

The Master's Son, 8½",
$65.00 – 75.00.

The Cousins, 11¾", $95.00 – 105.00.

Sophia, 11" x 11", has also been found 5½", $75.00 – 85.00.

Playmates, 9" x 9",
$75.00 – 85.00.

Peasant's Children, 7",
$55.00 – 60.00.

Belle's Blue Bonnet, 11¾",
$65.00 – 75.00.

Carla in a Cape, 7¾",
$55.00 – 65.00.

Baby Jane, 6½",
$50.00 – 60.00.

Poems, 7¾",
$55.00 – 65.00.

The Holy Day, 7¾",
$60.00 – 70.00.

The Bow, 7",
$60.00 – 70.00.

Fun Gathering Twigs, 9½",
$80.00 – 90.00.

Dancing the Reel, 9½",
$85.00 – 95.00.

Teeter-Totter, 9½",
$70.00 – 80.00.

The Student, 9½",
$100.00 – 110.00.

Be Mine, 9½",
$85.00 – 95.00.

Mommy's Girls, 9½",
$85.00 – 95.00.

The Goodbye Kiss, 6½" x 8½", $75.00 – 85.00.

The Waltz, 6½" x 9", $75.00 – 85.00.

The Painter, 9½", $90.00 – 100.00.

Mother's Helpers, 6½" x 8½", $50.00 – 60.00.

Teasing Old Nick, 4" x 5", $65.00 – 75.00.

We Better Leave Quick, 4" x 5", $65.00 – 75.00.

The Manuscript, 8", has also been found 9½", with a crimped frame, $65.00 – 75.00.

Adornment, 9½", $85.00 – 95.00.

The Countdown, 9½",
$85.00 – 95.00.

Fun on the Pond, 9½",
$85.00 – 95.00.

Winter Magic, 9½",
$85.00 – 95.00.

The Cherry Patch, 7" x 8",
$75.00 – 85.00.

The May Dance, 14",
$90.00 – 100.00.

Sister's Nap, 9¼",
$60.00 – 70.00.

Singing Trio, 8½" x 10",
$65.00 – 75.00.

Brother's Hug, 9¼",
$55.00 – 65.00.

A Visit to the Bell, 9" x 9", $60.00 – 70.00.

Fetching Water, 9¼", $55.00 – 65.00.

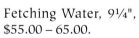

That Old Gang of Mine, 9½",
$90.00 – 100.00.

The Curls, 7¾",
$60.00 – 70.00.

Red Riding Hood and the Wolf, 9½", $90.00 – 100.00.

The Three Bears, 8½", $150.00 – 175.00.

A Visit to Grandmother's, 9½",
$90.00 – 100.00.

Children with Animals

Harmony, 9½",
$100.00 – 110.00.

Clara and Kitten, 9½",
$60.00 – 70.00.

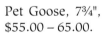
Pet Goose, 7¾",
$55.00 – 65.00.

The Reflection, 9½",
$100.00 – 110.00.

Baby Lambs, 7½",
$85.00 – 95.00.

My Friend Barney, 8",
$85.00 – 95.00.

Samantha's Kitten, 7¾",
$75.00 – 85.00.

Holding Felix, 4⅝",
$55.00 – 65.00.

Walking with Rover, 4⅝",
$55.00 – 65.00.

Petting the Lambs, 9¾",
$55.00 – 65.00.

Lydia and Hero, 7¾",
$90.00 – 100.00.

Holding Tiny Teddy, 9" x 9", $60.00 – 70.00.

Christmas

St. Nicholas, 10", $250.00 – 275.00.

Christmas Girl, 11¾",
$55.00 – 65.00.

Gatheringt the Greens, 9½",
$85.00 – 95.00.

The Marriage, 9½", $85.00 – 95.00.

His Intentions, 8½" x 10½", $60.00 – 70.00.

Over the Wall, 9½",
$55.00 – 65.00.

The Serenade, 10¼",
$50.00 – 60.00.

To the Market, 6¼",
$50.00 – 60.00.

Over the Fence, 9½",
$60.00 – 65.00.

After the Harvest, 9½", $60.00 – 65.00.

The Proposal, 7½" x 9", $50.00 – 60.00.

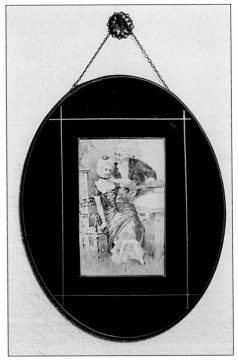

The Duet, 9½",
$50.00 – 60.00.

Courting, 11" x 11",
$50.00 – 60.00.

Under the Oak Tree, 9¼",
$55.00 – 65.00.

After the Dance, 9½",
$50.00 – 60.00.

The Royal Courtship, 9¼",
$85.00 – 95.00.

The Lute Player, 9½",
$85.00 – 95.00.

Strolling, 5¾",
$50.00 – 60.00.

Endearment, 5½",
$55.00 – 65.00.

Heaven's Pleasure, 8¾",
$85.00 – 95.00.

Mystery Beyond, 15½",
$110.00 – 120.00.

Please Stay, 15½",
$110.00 – 120.00.

Flowers

A Lovely Display, 9½",
$70.00 – 80.00.

A Box of Violets, 9½",
$75.00 – 85.00.

Pansies, 9½",
$75.00 – 85.00.

A Fall Display, 7" x 8¼", $75.00 – 85.00.

Roses Forever, 6½" x 8½", $55.00 – 65.00.

Pink Wisteria, 7" x 8¼",
$50.00 – 60.00.

Pink Wild Rose, 9¾",
$75.00 – 85.00.

Forget Me Nots, 9¾",
$75.00 – 85.00.

Lavender Wisteria, 9¾",
$55.00 – 65.00.

A Basket of Roses, 9½",
$85.00 – 95.00.

Red Roses in Vase, 8¼" x 7",
$85.00 – 95.00.

A Pretty Bouquet, 9½",
$85.00 – 95.00.

Pink Chrysanthemums,
9½", $85.00 – 95.00.

Bouquet's End, 8¼" x 7",
$85.00 – 95.00.

Pink and Red Roses, 9½",
$85.00 – 95.00.

Pink and Yellow Roses, 9½",
$85.00 – 95.00.

Yellow Daisies, 9½",
$85.00 – 95.00.

A Basket of Grapes, 8¼" x 6½", $75.00 – 85.00.

The Gift, 12", $75.00 – 85.00.

An Attractive Gift, 12",
$75.00 – 85.00.

A Hanging Basket, 9½",
$75.00 – 85.00.

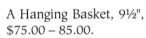

Pears on the Tree, 9½",
$75.00 – 85.00.

Ready to Pick, 9½",
$75.00 – 85.00.

A Tasty Treat, 7" x 8¼", $75.00 – 85.00.

Basket of Strawberries, 7" x 8¼", $75.00 – 85.00.

Blueberries and Tomatoes, 9½", $70.00 – 80.00.

Fruit and Nuts, 7¾", $75.00 – 85.00.

Oranges, 9½",
$80.00 – 90.00.

A Fall Delight, 10",
$65.00 – 75.00.

Grapes and Roses, 9½",
$85.00 – 95.00.

A Sweet Treat, 9½",
$85.00 – 95.00.

The Comforting, 9½", $75.00 – 85.00.

Grandpa's Story, 11¾", $90.00 – 100.00.

Roof Repairs, 6",
$50.00 – 60.00.

Rain, 11¼", has also
been found 11" x 11",
$75.00 – 85.00.

The Garland, 9½", $65.00 – 75.00.

Nature's Surprises, 9½", $85.00 – 95.00.

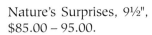

The Swing, 9½",
$85.00 – 95.00.

Summertime, 9½",
$85.00 – 95.00.

The Storm, 9½",
$85.00 – 95.00.

Oriental

Asian Beauty, 7",
$70.00 – 80.00.

The Parasol, 9½",
$50.00 – 60.00.

Flower Boy, 9½",
$50.00 – 60.00.

Halo of Roses, 9½",
$85.00 – 95.00.

Carmen, 9½",
$75.00 – 85.00.

Lisa's Coiffure, 9½",
$80.00 – 90.00.

Olivia,   9½",
$60.00 – 70.00.

The Musician, 8",
$60.00 – 70.00.

Hilda, 7¾",
$65.00 – 75.00.

Thinking, 7¾",
$55.00 – 65.00.

Susie,   8½",
$50.00 – 60.00.

Baltic Girl, 9½",
$55.00 – 65.00.

Innocence,   9½",
$75.00 – 85.00.

Bohemian Brunette, 9½", $90.00 – 100.00.

Lady in Red, 14", $150.00 – 175.00.

Lady with Iris, 9½", $85.00 – 95.00.

The Profile, 11", $55.00 – 65.00.

Frau and Frow, 9½",
$85.00 – 95.00.

Violet Lady, 7¾",
$50.00 – 60.00.

Juliana, 7¾",
$50.00 – 60.00.

Tresses, 7¾",
$55.00 – 65.00.

The Redhead, 7¾",
$55.00 – 65.00.

Almah, 7¾",
$50.00 – 60.00.

Garden Visit, 6¼" x 8", $55.00 – 65.00.

Mademoiselle, 9¼", $50.00 – 60.00.

The Bridesmaid, 4½",
$50.00 – 60.00.

The Gypsy, 11¾",
$95.00 – 105.00.

A White Bouquet, 7¾",
$75.00 – 80.00.

Feeding the Swallows,
8½", $65.00 – 75.00.

Posing, 10",
$65.00 – 75.00.

The Gossips, 7½" x 9",
$50.00 – 60.00.

Springtime, 8", $55.00 – 65.00.

The Wig, 6", $50.00 – 60.00.

Naive, 9¼",
$55.00 – 65.00.

The Flower Girl, 8½",
$55.00 – 65.00.

A Breath of Spring,
8½", also found 4" x
7¾", $55.00 – 65.00.

The Princess, 8½",
$55.00 – 65.00.

The Web, 9½", $85.00 – 95.00.

Lady with Fan, 9" x 9", has also been found 8", $50.00 – 60.00.

Woman with Children, 7¾"
$65.00 – 75.00.

The Father and
the Son, 7½",
$50.00 – 60.00.

Dreaming, signed Harrison Fischer–1910, 9½", $90.00 – 100.00.

Flapper, 7¾, $75.00 – 85.00.

Sophisticated Lady, signed G. Putikalery, 9¼", $90.00 – 100.00.

Garden Lady, 7½", $50.00 – 60.00.

A Host House by the Lake, 9" x 6¼", $50.00 – 60.00.

The Entrance, 9½", $55.00 – 65.00.

The Gateway, 9½",
$65.00 – 75.00.

Autumn, 8¼" x 6½",
$50.00 – 60.00.

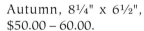

The Tulip Garden, 8¼" x 6¾", $50.00 – 60.00.

The Swans, 10¼", $70.00 – 80.00.

The Bungalow, 5¾",
$50.00 – 60.00.

The Waders,
6¾" x 8¾",
$50.00 – 60.00.

Market Day, 7½",
$50.00 – 60.00.

The Gleaners, 7¾",
$50.00 – 60.00.

Collecting Firewood, 8½" x 7"
$50.00 – 60.00.

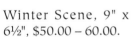
Winter Scene, 9" x
6½", $50.00 – 60.00.

Moose at the Lake, 7½",
$45.00 – 55.00.

House by the Creek,
10¼", $50.00 – 60.00.

A Walk through Town, 14", $85.00 – 95.00.

The Stone Bridge, 9½", $50.00 – 60.00.

Cottage by the Sea, 8",
$50.00 – 60.00.

The Clearing, 10",
$65.00 – 75.00.

The Fisherman, 9¼",
$60.00 – 70.00.

At the Well, 7",
$50.00 – 60.00.

The Vendor, 11½",
$60.00 – 70.00.

Feeding the Sheep, 7",
$50.00 – 60.00.

The Windmill, 8½",
$50.00 – 60.00.

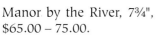

Manor by the River, 7¾",
$65.00 – 75.00.

River Town, 8½",
$65.00 – 75.00.

Casting the Nets, 6" x 5",
$50.00 – 60.00.

The Fur Muff, 7¾", $75.00 – 85.00.

The Matron, 9½", $90.00 – 100.00.

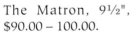

Ladykin, 9½",
$50.00 – 60.00.

The Feathered Chapeau, 6½" x 8¼",
$90.00 – 100.00.

Carlotta, 7¾",
$85.00 – 95.00.

The Rose Bonnet, 9½",
$90.00 – 110.00.

Fatima in Blue, 9½",
$90.00 – 110.00.

The Madam, 9½",
$90.00 – 100.00.

Summer Leisure, 9½",
$85.00 – 95.00.

Lena, 9½",
$85.00 – 95.00.

Priscilla, 9½",
$85.00 – 95.00.

Tattling to Mother, 9½",
$85.00 – 95.00.

Grand Dame, 9½",
$85.00 – 95.00.

The Ermine, 9½",
$85.00 – 95.00.

Zenobia, 9½",
$85.00 – 95.00.

The Wife, 6¾" x 8½",
$75.00 – 85.00.

Jezebel, 6½" x 8½", $75.00 – 85.00.

The Sweetheart, 7¾", $75.00 – 85.00.

Candice, 7¾",
$75.00 – 85.00.

Storytime, 9½",
$70.00 – 80.00.

Annalisse, 7½",
$85.00 – 95.00.

The Halo, 7½",
$85.00 – 95.00.

Therese, 7½",
$85.00 – 95.00.

Elizabeth, 9½",
$85.00 – 95.00.

Rita,   9½",
$80.00 – 90.00.

Willameana, 9½",
$80.00 – 90.00.

Victorian Beauty, 9½",
$90.00 – 110.00.

The Invitation, 9½",
$80.00 – 90.00.

Czarina, 9½",
$90.00 – 100.00.

Beatrice, 7",
$60.00 – 70.00.

Edward, 9",
$75.00 – 85.00.

Miscellaneous

Lariat Lassie, 9½",
$90.00 – 100.00.

The Country Maiden, 9½",
$90.00 – 100.00.

Flirting with
Fraulein, 6¼" x 8",
$55.00 – 65.00.

Nursing the Wounded, 6¼" x 6¼", $55.00 – 65.00.

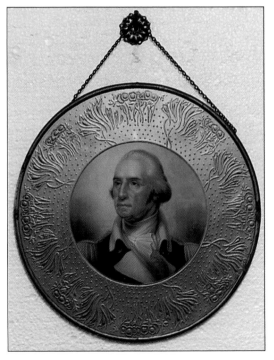

George Washington, 7¾", $60.00 – 70.00.

The Scholar, 8" x 10",
$80.00 – 90.00.

The Tavern, 8½",
$50.00 – 60.00.

Swallows, 9½", $85.00 – 95.00.

Schroeder's
ANTIQUES
Price Guide

. . . is the #1 best-selling
antiques & collectibles value guide on the market today,
and here's why . . .

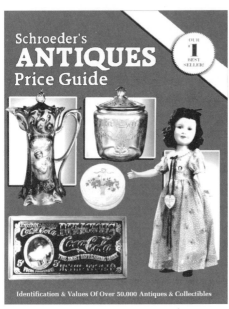

8½ x 11 • 608 Pgs. • PB • $12.95

• *More than 300 advisors, well-known dealers, and top-notch collectors work together with our editors to bring you accurate information regarding pricing and identification.*

• *More than 45,000 items in almost 500 categories are listed along with hundreds of sharp original photos that illustrate not only the rare and unusual, but the common, popular collectibles as well.*

• *Each large close-up shot shows important details clearly. Every subject is represented with histories and background information, a feature not found in any of our competitors' publications.*

• *Our editors keep abreast of newly developing trends, often adding several new categories a year as the need arises.*

If it merits the interest of today's collector, you'll find it in *Schroeder's*. And you can feel confident that the information we publish is up to date and accurate. Our advisors thoroughly check each category to spot inconsistencies, listings that may not be entirely reflective of market dealings, and lines too vague to be of merit. Only the best of the lot remains for publication.

Without doubt, you'll find
SCHROEDER'S ANTIQUES
PRICE GUIDE
the only one to buy for
reliable information and values.

COLLECTOR BOOKS
A Division of Schroeder Publishing Co., Inc.